Friendl

SINGLE POETS
SERIES

§

urban biology

ian gibbins

§

Friendly Street Poets

Friendly Street Poets Incorporated
PO Box 3697
Norwood
South Australia 5067
friendlystreetpoets.org.au

Wakefield Press
1 The Parade West
Kent Town
South Australia 5067
www.wakefieldpress.com.au

First published 2012

Cover and inside artwork copyright © Judy Morris
Cover design by Ian Gibbins
Edited by Thom Sullivan, Friendly Street Poets
Typeset by Clinton Ellicott, Wakefield Press
Printed in Australia by Griffin Digital, Adelaide

National Library of Australia Cataloguing-in-Publication entry

Author: Gibbins, Ian.
Title: Urban biology / Ian Gibbins.
ISBN: 978 1 74305 099 6 (pbk.).
Series: Friendly Street single poets series.
Subjects: Australian poetry – 21st century.
Dewey Number: A821.4

Government
of South Australia
Arts SA

Friendly Street Poets Inc. is supported by the **South Australian Government** through **Arts SA**.

fox creek
wines

Ian Gibbins is a neuroscientist and Professor of Anatomy and Histology at Flinders University, having originally trained in zoology and pharmacology. He is internationally recognised for his research on the microscopic structure and function of the nerves that monitor and control the activity of the internal organs. He teaches a variety of topics and has had significant input into the design and implementation of Flinders' innovative Graduate Entry Medical Program, winning several teaching awards.

In recent years, Ian's poems have appeared in a range of publications, including *Best Australian Poems 2008*, and have been shortlisted in several national poetry competitions. He has contributed text to installations around Adelaide and to Australian Dance Theatre's 2010 Adelaide Festival of Arts production, *Be Your Self*. He also regularly reviews science books for *Australian Book Review*. Ian's spoken word and electronic music have been published in *Going Down Swinging* and *Cordite* and broadcast on ABC Radio National. His sound videos have featured in South Australian Living Artists' Moving Image program. He collaborates closely with artists in public events to promote the common ground between art and science. He is also an avid windsurfer …

www.iangibbins.com.au

Acknowledgments

First and foremost, big thanks to Friendly Street Poets for the strong and supportive environment they provide for poets of every ilk. Their publication program is a key element of their activity and I am both delighted and honoured to be selected for the Single Poets series. Special thanks to Thom Sullivan and Maggie Emmett of Friendly Street Poets for their support and advice in getting this book together.

Many people have encouraged and helped my writing in various ways, but I particularly thank Linda Cooper, Marcello Costa, Teresa Crea, Maggie Emmett, Sally Francis, Erica Jolly, Janice Lally, Natasha Mitchell, Peter Rose, Garry Stewart, Ronnie Taheny, Catherine Truman and Chris Wallace-Crabbe, for providing unique opportunities to inspire, critique and present my work. Much of what appears in this volume would not have happened without them. I also acknowledge the positive influence of the editors of poetry journals and judges of poetry competitions: they are faced with a task of extraordinary difficulty. I am always grateful whenever my words manage to survive their selection processes and I enjoy learning from the works of those who succeed ahead of me.

Urban Biology is strongly informed by science, science that is rigorous, rational and mechanistic, yet suffused with wonder and respect. I am indebted to the extraordinary environments of the Department of Zoology, University of Melbourne, where I was a student, and the School of Medicine, Flinders University, where I have worked since 1985, for supporting my efforts in the quest for understanding just how this world of ours works.

Special thanks to Judy Morris, who, amongst everything else, has provided the beautiful illustrations for this book. You see more of her stunning work at www.judymorris.net.au. The 'we' in these poems most often refers to us.

Many poems in this collection have been published or otherwise made available in the public domain: 'Kites' and parts of 'With Body in Mind (After Vesalius)' in *Corridors*; 'Field Guide' in *Australian Book Review* (short-listed for poetry prize, 2007) and *Best Australian Poems 2008*; 'Beanie on the Moon', 'Dead Dog (Subtitled)', 'Window Seats' and 'Mutton Birds, ANZAC Day' in various *Friendly Street Poets Readers*; 'Esplanade' and 'Middle of the Road' in *Blast*; 'Types of Rain' in *Going Down Swinging*; 'Space Invaders' and 'Taboo' in *Transnational Literature*; 'Rules for Interior Design' and 'Love Falters at Darling Harbour' in *Blue Dog*; 'Turtledove', 'Lullabies, Gardens Road Cemetery', 'Local Knowledge' and 'Shuffle' in *Page Seventeen* (all competition finalists, 2008, 2010); 'Letter to Nature, 21st January, 2010' in *Newcastle Poetry Prize 2010*; 'Amazing Grace' and 'First Week of Winter' on-line for the *Max Harris Poetry Prize* (short-list and high commendation, respectively, 2008, 2009); 'The Science of Shark Fishing' on-line for *Friendly Street Poets Poem of the Month*; 'ecg' in *Challenging the Divide* by Erica Jolly (2010), part of *Heartsong* installations at Flinders Medical Centre and the Science Exchange, RiAus, Adelaide, 2009, and broadcast on ABC Radio National's *All in the Mind*, 2008, 2009; 'Thoracic' as part of *Not Absolute* exhibition / installation at Flinders University City Gallery, 2009; 'Abbess Chiara, Montefalco, 1308', 'According to Grey's (Meredith Lives)' and 'The Boy with Two Bodies' performed with videos and podcast as part of *Anatomy & Imagination* at the Science Exchange, RiAus, Adelaide, 2010; 'Dr Korsakoff and Colleagues Report' in *Southerly* (2012).

Contents

For JM,
lifetime collaborator in the science,
art and romance of Urban Biology.

Space Invaders

Dropping in from 12 o'clock high,
you will barely notice our arrival.
Being neither green
nor of unduly small stature,
we blend easily
with the streetwise procession
of Friday night diners, party goers
and good-natured drunks.

Once we are here,
molecule by precious molecule,
we will infiltrate your haemopoietic stream,
until your body fluids flow as thin as solar wind.
Like bamboo beneath your fingernails,
we will reduce all communication
to compromise and distant comets,
adrift in the cloying starlight.

Already you can see the places we have been:
the sea cliffs fallen away,
ocean currents reversed,
corals faded to desert stone
and cyclones following our path
across land-locked harbours,
over clouded mountain ranges,
to your humble fragile abodes.

But for the moment
we are sitting unsighted
behind the silvered glass of the Spiegel Tent:
where now are the acrobats?
the tumblers?
the flying trapeze?
where now the sawdust?
the tattoos and scars?

For the moment, we imagine
the quiet hum of an air conditioner
bathing us with cool relief,
redolent with strawberries,
raspberries, milk-sapped figs,
the welcome fruits of your earth.
For the moment, as you can imagine,
we are sitting pretty.

Amazing Grace

If we were in the spotlight,
I did not notice. If there were
loudspeakers and megaphones,
I did not listen.

There were, however,
fields of sugarcane. Yes.
The juice fresh and clear and
sticky on our fingers and lips
and matting our unkempt hair;
like grit-ash between our toes,
the stinging cuts on our feet,
it would linger for days with
our sweat and the itchiness
in our skin, until the rain,
yes, the rain finally fell and
hit the ground and we wept
and washed and closed
our thankful eyes to Heaven.

Almost certainly, there were
cotton plantations and corn.
Yes. The husks dried, rustling,
the wings of beetles, snakes
black and lingering, tongues
aflicker, warning us to
stay away, to be wary
of where we should tread,
of where we should hide
and cower and speak in low
tones, bodies close to the earth,
to each other, to the dust
that covered us, for just a
moment or two, with silence.

Then there was the storm,
the winds and hounds, wailing,
and widows. Yes. Widows, as
palings clapped and tore loose
and the air filled with flood
so dark, so hard, we could
no longer stand, we could
no longer hold on, and
the trees fell fast and were
lost in the current, and when
day finally broke, finally broke,
and we found our hands
and our hearts still beating,
all you could hear was the

drawing of breath, yes,
the drawing of breath,
how sweet the sound,
how sweet the sound.

Love Falters at Darling Harbour

'… alternatively, we could walk to the Maritime Museum.'

She hugged him, kissed him. He looked
down, counted the red-brick pavers between
his shoelaces and the concourse seagulls.

And the answer? It depends: wide angle or
long shot, polariser on or off, shutter speed,
flash synchronisation, status of the battery charge.

Was this in the social contract? Was this the
expectation when names were first exchanged?
And the answer? Twenty-eight, give or take.

Twenty-nine? The bollards, at least. A decent
place to think about nothing, observe the woman
cocooned with yellow silk, an avatar or two,

practise untrained legerdemain, loosen
frayed ropes of spellbound misunderstanding,
misappropriated glances, subliminal attraction.

Maybe he could taste something in her sweat.
Maybe there was some electrostatic force, like
lightning conductors or black cat fur before a storm.

Would babies be involved? Don't they look
the same? Don't they sound the same? Don't they
smell of butterflies and booties and sour spilt milk?

A coin toss, for all it matters, a badly dealt card.
But did she notice? A bird with one leg? Digital
or analog? A submarine? A replica? And if someone

slipped? Too many questions without notice. But
if his brakes were to fail? The surface of the water?
How to move sideways? Is this, or was that, an ending?

ecg

light hearted
heavy hearted
soft hearted
broken hearted
heartache

open hearted
cold hearted
empty hearted
kind hearted
heart of gold

goodness of your heart
bottom of my heart
heartfelt
heartless
change of heart

lion hearted
stout hearted
heart like an ox
your heart's desire
learnt by heart

hale and hearty
his hearty laugh
her hearty broth
heartburn
your heart on your sleeve

down hearted
faint hearted
bleeding heart
heartened to hear
the heart of the matter

sweetheart
this heartland
this heart of the country
this heartbeat
this heart to heart.

Travel Plans

'Stay in your lane,' she muttered.
The smell of crushed metal
followed us like tyre-tracks,
like the feeling of sniffer dogs
fussing around my ankles,
as if I had contraband in my socks
or crumbs of mutton sandwiches
in my grandfather's Gladstone bag.

She mentioned something about
rugby players, or maybe ten-ton
trucks, semi-trailers, B-doubles,
a road train. The radio faltered.
Once more we were reduced
to talkback, arguments about
bicycle lanes, underpasses,
overpasses, implicit rights of way.

Tasmania was a good idea.
So was Uluru. But with our
rear-vision flashing, kaleidoscopic,
good ideas simply disappeared
into the runoff, just so much
stormwater, running through
the floodways, our personal
contributions to climate change.

Lullabies, Gardens Road Cemetery

Through the stillness you invoke when the traffic goes quiet,
when the wind falls calm and leaves quiver but do not drop,
you may convince yourself: 'Yes, I can hear them.' Perhaps

flowers might have been folded from tissue paper or Chinese silk;
a plaque might once have been a ploughshare, perhaps only one
breath, only one name, unaccompanied, only 'Tom', unadorned.

Yes, perhaps you can hear them: hushed below widow-maker gums,
buttressed figs, under tussocks, dandelions, iron wrought by sadness,
these wistful strains, the lullabies of the barely born, a mother's song,

after Father, finally, unremittingly, never returned; perhaps you
can hear her incantation, embedded in oxide and earth, whispered
on this eternal November the fifth, nineteen hundred and forty-six.

Departing the Gardens, perhaps you can ignore hints of gristle, caul,
marrow, sinew. Perhaps you can ask a translation of polished marble.
Perhaps, out of silence, you can tally the miles old lullabies have slept.

Kites

There's one
and there, another:
black shouldered kites,
almost certainly a pair
uncharacteristically struggling
to hold position
against the blustery nor'wester
against (to use the weatherman's words)
the anticyclonic gloom.

On the other side of the main South Road,
I find it difficult to explain
why I am still wearing sunglasses.
I find it difficult to explain
why my baby won't stop crying.
But for now, I have only two questions:
will the rain wash the dye from my hair?
and
when will the bus come?

Dead Dog (subtitled)

No, not yet,
not as long as we are counting dog years
(or blue moons, faded, desaturated, pale
almost to transparency, almost to the sky's limit,
calling us to howl at the very end of space).

When spring tides peak
high at two metres, two point five, two point six
(it's that kind of day when land's edge slides
away from footfall, folded back through wavelets,
abating sea breezes, unfurled sailcloth echoes).

Until ten
in the morning, dogs may run on the beach
(off the leash, should we so desire, should we
be overtaken by the urge to race, to hunt, to dig
and scratch and roll, to dive, or jump up and fly).

As long as we
are counting dog years, there still might be time
(to learn one more new trick, to continue to breathe
ozone sunrises in old and familiar company, still time
to glimpse another blue moon, just before she scuttles).

Shuffle

Although I am surrounded by row after row of deckchairs,
this (most decidedly) is not anywhere on the *Titanic*.
No icebergs here, unless you count the lettuce, wilted
(browning in shreds), beside hamburger wrappers and
(not quite) emptied *Toohey's Red* or *New*, abandoned
(surprisingly) after a night of who-knows-what may have
happened, once the pubs were shut, the clubs (finally)
had secured their double-steel-skinned doors, when one

(or two) of us slipped headlong into muscle-bound narcosis,
to be roused (luckily, in the end) by street-sweeper gears,
crickets crushed underfoot, else (failing that) the whoops
(if not hollers) from dawn-broken swimmers, full of praise
for the warm-as-toast sun and (can we say?) born-again
light in Pacific swells, pulsing with more than enough
energy to sink any ship's captain so foolish (so careless!)
as to ignore such latitudinous signs of forthcoming inclemency.

Reasons for Remaining Earthbound

One: Feet planted firmly on the ground
    Running off at tangents,
    we find it hard to keep to time.

    Running off at tangents,
    we reverse contact with earth and air.

    Running off at tangents,
    our words of greeting drift apart.

Two: Grass growing between the toes
    We have always regarded
    the waltz as something special,
    but, this time, it doesn't seem right.

    Still, we await the rain …
    There are no birds.
    Where are the birds?

Three: The unyielding effects of gravity
    We are escapees
    from the longest night.

    Far beyond the ecliptic,
    where else can we go?

Four: Sighs from behind a hidden door
    All sweetness
    and floral aromatics,
    aware but not alert,

    I didn't know
    how bad it was
    until I tried to speak.

Five: Turns of phrase, figures of speech
>Hand to hand,
>we stroll along boulevards and riverbanks,
>we spin among swirling chorus lines.
>
>Hand to mouth,
>we pass our stories, our delectable histories,
>another, another, beyond unfamiliar horizons.
>
>Mouth to mouth,
>we kiss, we intermingle, we breathe
>life into this, our common land.

Probably a Sacrifice

I cannot tell you the manner of my death.
After all these centuries in the bog, the peat,
the deep encompassing darkness,
the enveloping mists and moss,
I have no knowledge, it is beyond my ken.

After all these centuries, I wonder
how it is, how it was, what difference
one more breath might have made,
the songs I might have sung,
the poems and sermons I might have heard.

After all these centuries, the sun
is more intense than I remember:
I must close my eyes to the unaccustomed glare;
I must retreat from the flashes and incandescent
counter-lighting floods you aim in my direction.

After all these centuries, I cannot walk away
from this place of outcasts and disembodied sprites:
my sandals and ceremonial capes have been purloined;
my feet, swathed in pristine cotton, linger in the distance,
errant, beyond the power of my will.

The band around my neck is no longer tight.
After all these centuries, its leather plaits,
its strangling knots no longer cut my flesh.
Protected by my cap and your soft-gloved hands,
this simply is how I have come to rest.

Man with a Broken Tooth

He replied with a characteristic lisp,
not usually associated with a man
of his undeniable power and influence.

There had been a fight, or maybe,
as claimed in the sporting pages,
a series of pugilistic incidents.

> Lizards scuttled for cover,
> tails coiled, breath held.
> Crickets stilled, waited, silent.

They were hot nights, tight with
build-up and electrical tension,
thundering, ready to explode.

Someone had cash; others, concealed
weapons; yet another aimed cameras
through finger-streaked windows.

> Flying foxes filled the dusk,
> stole the scent of ripe mango,
> left a trail of moonprints.

Passers-by agreed: screams followed,
gunshots came first, and after it all,
a hailstorm of shattered glass.

Eye-witnesses put him at the scene,
fairly, squarely, in the centre of the action.
It obviously was him, they said.

> Did you see the crocodile?
> they asked. Did you meet its
> golden stare, its inviting gape?

You easily could tell, they said.
His teeth gave him away. His tooth
was broken, they said, at the root.

His words hiss across the tip of his tongue.
His words pass the point of no return.
His words will neither confirm nor deny.

      Blowflies, locusts, hunting spiders:
      is this the plague upon us?
      Is he the one we should blame?

He says others see darkness, a void,
old damaged merchandise. He says
he sees the rewards of waylaid trust.

It is time. There is no further comment.
Electronics cool. His grin withdraws,
sneers, into diamond-hard incandescence.

      A snake was in the grass, they said,
      a viper on the breast, a boa, they said,
      constricted around his heart.

Home Pharmacy

Reckitt's Blue
Let me hang a piece of sky below the place where
voice sweeps and soars, when time turns away,

when snowlight surrounds the part of an eye where
nothing is reflected but luminous prismatic desire.

Mercurochrome
A winged messenger carries you boldly past
perihelion, an orbit uncalculated, extreme,

and in a flash, your apple-fine skin splits,
burns, vermillion, scarlet, crimson; the stuff

within your veins, part quicksilver, part iron,
falters, transforms, to sheer diaphanous vapour.

Elemental Sulphur
Could it be that, already, I have plumbed
the deepest fulminating bowels of the earth?

Could it actually be that, already, I have ground
pumice and brimstone into dust so fine as to

infiltrate my speech, to smother any signs
of life from my words; a dust so astringent,

so desiccating, as to sere the back of my throat
tinderbox dry, kindled to ignite, to spit flame

like a dragon, feverishly breaking cover, defiant,
unblooded, awaiting one final thrust and parry?

Tincture of Iodine
Picture my limbs wrapped, deliciously entwined with
seaweed, frond upon frond of bladderwrack, bull kelp,

Neptune's Necklace, as if I were a stealthy leviathan,
unmarked, unremarked, dipping in and out of view,

trailing eddies, wakes, vortices, the come and go with each
release of breathhold, almost too long, almost at the point

where shooting stars swarm, explode, into diamond dust,
heedlessly distant from any lighthouse or emergency beacon.

Clove Oil
While my mouth fills with icicles, only an improbable
alignment of planets can conjure up the type of atmospheric

perturbation that would see backyards and parkways lush around
polar lava flows, anaesthetic with unseasonable

mangoes, pawpaws, lychees, and these luxuriant opiates,
these gorgeous, aromatic, barely enmorphed spectres.

Gentian Violet
Somewhere here, there, a little to the left, a little
to the right, up a fraction, down a fraction, the itch

you scratch with carefully measured arcs, the itch you
satisfy, you soothe, far beyond drifting ultramarine.

According to Grey's (Meredith Lives)

As long as the labels are green,
sterility is guaranteed: your disbelief
will not convince me otherwise.

Later, we may well celebrate,
but I will ignore, I promise,
your hand, light on my shoulder,

the curl of your tongue,
the carefully rehearsed
arching of your eyebrows.

I will continue to grit my teeth
and, as though sinking under
ice, cracking, reforming ice,

I will take any small advantage
offered by sub-zero temperatures
until I drift back, further

behind jibs and spinnakers,
cinematic curtains,
parachute silk,

billowing, floating away
from your radiographic
lines of sight, finally

outside the range
of your scalpels, retractors,
your painlessly dissolving sutures.

Middle of the Road

This is nothing like
magnolias floating in a bowl of mercury

schools of flying-fish beneath
a glittering Tommy Ruff sky

conversations between spider orchids
barely audible through the thornbrush

barely audible through
the tangle of cassette tapes

the twisted telephone wires
the finger-picked notes

folded, refolded
in the glove-box of my car.

This is nothing like
the broken white line

that divides my fluttering attention
that stills the butterflies

barely audible, trapped
within the pit of my stomach.

Taboo

Why should we be smiling?
After all, we are displaced
from our country, our lands,
our mothers and fathers,
our brothers and our sisters.

Why should we reveal to you,
through your staring, brass-rimmed lens,
what we think of your horses and carts,
those trinkets, the royal insignia
that adorn your epaulettes and coattails?

We know what will happen when you leave:
we cooperate under sufferance,
taking advantage of argentic shade,
the hills and riven valleys, subjugating
the light you require, so precisely aligned,

so perfectly diffused, to capture us,
to frame us, for a second or two,
to hang us, with your reflections,
congregated, along the walls of your museums,
your archives and acquisitive collections.

Why should we be smiling?
After all, we have been displaced.
We have been spirited away.
According to law, our eyes must close:
according to law, we may never look back.

Notes on the Weather

Explanation of the surface chart
Skirting above the isobars,
our wingtips scythe across
your time-zone, your sunset,
falling in evanescent waves
like a pilgrim's robes, like
rose petals fading beyond
earth-warmed invisibility.

Fireban advice
From neighbour
to nearest neighbour,
join wild divergent
drumbeats,
re-enter solar flares,
tattoo lovingly feathered
dendritic space.

Coastal waters forecast
An escape from the heat,
I will slide inverted, myopic,
into this looking-glass sea,
into these slashing
barbed-wire arms, these
patiently gathering
medusae.

Road weather alert
When temperature gradients reverse,
when we breed all too quickly,
when we associate one with another,
with red-billed zebra-finches,
with such an improbable gene-pool,
when snowmelt flicks from our
plumage and fingers and eyelashes.

For those of you travelling interstate
Most mornings you can peer past
storm-bleached coral banks, see
distant western hinterlands blush,
mirror pomegranates, persimmons.
But, today, blue trevally runs and
catamarans blur, sublime, reform,
unshadowed, fogbound, irresolute.

Update on climate change
Ultimately the fate of thylacines,
the things that may yet be lost:
the future predicates new models.
New supermarkets? New hospitals?
Hence the gaps? The unanticipated
benefits? Thus we trawl the oceans,
the dry subcontinental escarpments.

The extended outlook
Everywhere the ants, the ants,
crowding gravelly walkways,
recurved blades of grass,
until the hot low sky engulfs us,
until the first drops of rain
silence our halting speech,
electrify our points of departure.

Sounds of the Sea

Earache: just so much flotsam, jetsam, ankle-deep around trouser cuffs, unspecified questions, echoes of Pacific gulls, storm-petrels, fairy prions.

Earbud: coquette, cockle, shell-like, for example:
'Is this where your heart lies?'

Eardrum: probably an illusion, taken within smoke, drawn goat-skin tight, once monsoon rains pass.

Earhole: the evolutionary equivalent of catching one's breath, a predilection for secrets.

Earlobe: mother of pearl, fleeting phosphorescence, trails through rockpools, hand across mouth, a revelation.

Earplug: neither *Marshall* nor *Stax*, vacuum tubes that sway beneath coconut palms, too far from breaking waves, rips, rushing sand.

Earring: a mass approaching death by drowning, an incorruptible promise enclosed by at least one cable-knit shroud of recognition.

Eartip: formerly entangled algal mats, now respite after a storm, gales, singular.

Earwax: spermaceti (?), ambergris (?), perfume persistent, ill-defined, distant, carried on stray Antarctic winds.

Earwig: here, two points, or rather, scrimshaw dust falling away as moonflakes on a receding tide.

Earworm: the period of a swell, circumpolar depression, foundless allure, remembered only from time to time.

Abbess Chiara, Montefalco, 1308

'... her body should be preserved on account of her holiness and because God took such pleasure in her body and heart ... After vespers or thereabouts, the said Francesca, Margherita, Lucia and Caterina went to get the heart, which was in a box ... And the said Francesca of Foligno cut open the heart with her own hand and opening it they found in the heart a cross, or the image of the crucified Christ.'

SISTER FRANCESCA OF FOLIGNO (1318)

Understand that we, your Sisters, do this
out of respect for the truth of your testimony.

Understand that we do this
out of love and dedication,

that we acknowledge
the gifts of heavenly grace

bestowed upon you
beyond your material desires,

freed of devilish contrivance
or fabrication or calumny.

So forgive us, dear Sister,
as we peel back your incorruptible skin

like the petals of a flower
barely touched by this morning's sun.

Forgive us, dear Sister,
when we expose your maw,

when we cover your sinews
with herbs and fragrant spices

like a tender young lamb
ready for the fire.

Please, forgive us, dear Sister
once we have cleaved

your unkissed breast
and found the evidence for God

encased so securely within
your miraculous, blameless heart.

Mary Docherty, Edinburgh, 1828

The last victim of William Burke and William Hare,
notorious procurers of fresh bodies for the Edinburgh School
of Anatomy.

How remarkable it is
after all this time,
despite my lowly station,
my miserable and uneventful life,
you still talk about me,
you still know my name.

My miserable and uneventful life;
my wayward, my errant son.
Why else visit this drear stonegrit town?
Why else would I succumb once again
to miasmic devils and spirits
bewitched by riffling midnight vapours?

I might then have missed that William Burke,
his hands around my soused old voice-box,
his hands covering my wrinkled hide with straw,
his hands selling me for the anatomist's knife,
his hands lifted to God Almighty
in preparation for that final drop.

By now, the townsfolk have had their skimmington,
they have shouted and marched
through the Surgeon's Square,
they have seen revealed upon the table
the raw and bloody entrails
of death traded for unholy death.

Of course, nothing I can say will change
the minds of those choleric soft-palmed toffs,
who reap profit from our thankless labour,
whose one grand speech after another
punish the walls of Parliament, whose pronouncements
reek with the stink of the Poor House.

Perhaps, after all, you can appreciate
that I only dreamt of Ireland,
of the chances I could have taken,
of the life I might not have lost.
Perhaps, after all, you can appreciate
that I wish you have never heard of me.

Turtledove

What if we think of her
as a stowaway, transported
like a common criminal
or illegal immigrant,
burdened with nothing
but hazy dreams, in this
foundling land of errant
meridians, stretched beyond
the limits of navigation?

What if we think of her
skies, rent by whistling
shadows, a beating wake,
by the goshawk, ready
to drop, to end flight, to
dull the hand-me-down
jewels, the diamantes,
that ring her unsuspecting,
unprotected neck?

Heart Dissection
for BJG

1. Cardiac Output
Circularity: at least a working definition,
approximating squared radii, right angles
cubed, bevelled off, transformed to flows,

pulsing like the seasons, like the muscles
of seabirds migrating the length of the earth.
Meanwhile, our unreefed, unerased futures,

gather round architectural drawings, replete
with promises of a new roof over our heads,
a view away from fire-scarred hills towards

the coastal verge, towards each change in
pressure, each not-quite-timely reminder,
that enlivens our inexplicably recurrent past.

2. Conducting System
Through reciprocating harmonic series,
I gladly give to you:
bundles of hopeful predilection,

woven cords of neighbourliness,
rows of intercalated desire,
the trigger-happy rush of escape,

bands of enthusiastic light and dark,
a perfect cup of tea,
your waiting next of kin.

3. Septum

On the other side,
there is a tangible sense of barely sullied air.

On the other side,
the observable spectrum shifts to markedly longer wavelengths.

On the other side,
expectation matches the potential for renewal.

On the other side,
strange attractors let loose magnificent unrehearsed adventure.

4. Venous Return

We travelled to Jupiter, circled
Galileo's moons (Io and Europa,
Ganymede, Callisto) swirling,
roiling, like the mighty Red Spot,
three thousand million feet below.

We navigated vast oceans, tacked
from meridian to meridian. Boldly
indifferent to seductive doldrums or
looming sub-equatorial storms, we
snared luscious, fat-lipped, coral trout.

We crossed the Great Sandy Desert,
the Gobi, the Sahara, dug for water,
for evidence, a lasting trace, for ancestors,
lobe-finned, ephemeral, and beside them,
settled under arid counter-paned skies.

Now we relax around campfires,
embers cool, ironwood smoking
ghosts, exchanging natural histories,
as seas fall calm and planets sink
beneath far-off indigo mountains.

Can we delineate the conditions
that bring us here? Can we hope to
calibrate our co-ordinates, to specify
the sum of our explorations, the grand
total of our arrivals, our departures?

Behind us, again, the subtle force
to move on, just a feint, just a gentle
nudge in the back. So we do, so we do,
until once more beyond our zenith,
we track the tumbling moons of Jupiter.

With Body in Mind (After Vesalius)

1: Preparator
Surrounded by rows of knuckles
boiled and bleached free of their marrow
I focus through my lenses
to place facet on articulated facet
and with a skeleton of surprise, I reconstruct
this intimation of a beating heart.

In preparation for display
my texts and numbered charts are closed,
the cabinet door locked shut;
under the magnifying beams of spotlights,
I polish my glass eyes
and stitch my skin tight around me.

2: Students
Once the paperwork is done
the rest is just formality

an irredeemable end
to caged silences of a lifetime

precisely at the tip of a scalpel
this he, this she

when cool with missing breath
we look on and look away.

3: Donors

No-one is likely to argue
that, any time soon,
we will be moving far from here.

Not because our bones
have become soft and yellow,
carefully exposed

below these anonymous cotton sheets.
Nor because our nerves,
now slack, without tension or tone,

no longer sing like piano strings.
Nor even because our
rich red blood and

dark shining muscles
have ceased to pump, to pulse.
As you can see, we are done with action:

all we have left is intent and desire;
all we wish is for
you to feel our warmth.

Field Guide

1 Preface
I could, if you prefer, create a list
like a birdwatcher, concealed
in a reedy hide, with binoculars,
field guide and record book, a mnemonic
of migration lines, our lines of sight,
a cladogram of our evolving past.

2.1 Comb jellies (Ctenophora)
Our nerve net
pulsing
invisible
our eightfold
metachronic prisms
ripple through the rain of light.

2.2 Spotted eagle rays (Myliobatridae)
If we had feet, we would dance;
if we had hands, we would hold them.
Instead, we reel and dip our leisurely trefoils.
We have stars on our backs;
they travel with us,
untouchable reflections of an untouched sky.

2.3 Parrot fish (Scaridae)
With all their fancy feathers
I suppose the lorikeets and rosellas
can be as brash and noisy as they like.
I would rather take my time
and, gliding between the staghorns,
arrive in rainbowed silence.

2.4 Hawksbill turtle (Chelonidae)
Down here among the soft corals,
the ocean moves less.
Ever so slowly, I eke out my oxygen,
await the incoming tide
to clear their unguents, their crèmes,
and salve my shadow-sharp eyes.

3.1 Blue tigers (Nymphalidae)
Somewhere between the clouds and the earth
unaccountable corridors of attraction lure us,
tasting the eddies and wakes of falling leaves,
of the trails left by every one of us,
until we metamorphose, finally, into cool
ether streams, veiled with weeping mists.

3.2 Black fruit bats (Pteropodidae)
This would be a great place to hang around
making bad puns and not much better jokes,
were it not for the mosquitoes, thirteen to the dozen,
twisting and turning us back to front
and upside down, the webs between our fingers
itching in expectation of sweet and sticky flight.

4.1 Sooty shearwater (Procellariidae)
You really have to agree
that when the southeast trades blow so hard,
when the air stings with so much salt
that the sun turns as white as a pearl,
when the landlost cry for their atropine and ginger,
you can see all the way to Alaska.

4.2 Striped dolphins (Delphinidae)
We have no knowledge of aerodynamics,
fluid flow, or the diffusion of soluble gasses,
but from below the clicking interface of our sonar horizon,
we jump
we jump
we jump.

5 Index
Awash on the reef,
calcareous impressions,
days at an end,
enforced retreat,
quiet taxonomy,
secret unhurried returns.

Window Seats

It always has struck me as odd
that the cabin crew so diligently show us
how to use a life vest, when the whole flight
is over land, with barely enough water to catch
a geometer's reflections of the tracking sun.
But as we cross the Equator, eight miles
above the breaking swells of the Pacific Ocean,
for once, it doesn't seem such a bad idea.

From the vapid smell-drift of sleep and coffee, a faint
scent of familiarity envelops my allocated space.
Naturally, I recognise it is not yours.
(How much do they sell in a year of duty free?)
In any case, the curling tendrils of perfume
draw me out of my seat and closer to home,
to streets lined purple with November jacarandas,
to our shared, all-embracing air.

First Week of Winter

i

Standing in the shower, water hot,
thick like Mallee honey on my back,
a mass of earth, the mass of the earth,
washed away, blood, paling, thin, drains
to my feet, from my ears, under shaking
hands, full of whispers or thunderclaps,
muffled bird calls, rattling gumnuts:
is this what it's like when there's
no spring, no summer? Is this
what it's like when days lengthen
no more beyond glimpses of wattles
in bud, promises of roasted almonds,
an eagle, a kestrel, soaring, searching?

ii

When we reached the river sands,
we were surprised not by buttress roots,
exposed, cracked, lined by ebbs and floods
never counted, never measured, never
aware of our arrival, of our time, here;
we were surprised not by rain falling
behind us, removing drop by drop
any lasting clue that might indicate,
should we turn, should we follow a
misplaced word or two, another way home;
amongst bulrushes and shadows of mistletoe,
our eyes touched with a familiarity we were
surprised to recognise, surprised to accept.

iii

Even meteorologists admit such cloud
formations are seen so rarely they remain
undocumented, unclassified, unnamed:
there is no word for a segment of rainbow,
detached, drifting free of its arc; there is no
word for an atmospheric surge, a receding tide
of light and not quite dark; there is no word
for the distance between contact with songs
almost inaudible, with arms almost linked,
with footfalls almost dancing, and a peak
of cumulonimbus, rising, rolling, almost
disappearing, obscuring sky and sea and
land beyond honey and rivers and rainbows.

Types of Rain

1. Outside the range of normal atmospheric conditions:
    - *(a)*   recently discovered caves
    - *(b)*   fine Martian dust
    - *(c)*   water columns, three kilometres deep;

2. Accordingly, when unexpected illuminations appear:
    - *(d)*   last over before stumps
    - *(e)*   birthday cakes
    - *(f)*   parades, a wedding gown parade;

3. When no-one seems to be looking:
    - *(g)*   another tin roof
    - *(h)*   monsoon season
    - *(i)*   click-beetles, longicorns, scarabs;

4. When no-one seems to be listening:
    - *(j)*   rivulets on the kitchen door glass
    - *(k)*   grevilleas in flower
    - *(l)*   feathers, from a crimson rosella;

5. When, nevertheless, falling:
    - *(m)*   like fruit, a little overripe
    - *(n)*   like lips to your silence
    - *(o)*   like mist, leaving your eyes and mine.

Local Knowledge

About now, I reckon,
according to the current flows,
the seasonal drifts and eddies,
the atmospheric gradients,
barometric pressures,
sea-surface temperatures,
the passing phases of the moon,
about now, according to local knowledge,
the tide should be at its lowest ebb.

About now, I reckon,
we should have an hour or so
to continue our path along the land's edge,
to drag our feet through halogenic skeins of weed,
our toenails packed with sand,
our shins salty with foaming wavespray,
our hands clasped together as tight as oyster shells
that hide, according to local knowledge,
precious pearls within.

Apparition

1. Greenwood, Western Australia, 2003

The sun was setting and the dogs were barking – the dog
was barking – and the wind was full of Light and we stopped
and stared. The wind was full of Light and, praise the Lord,
it twisted and turned like my fingers around the Rosary
and the animals, the animals, all the Lord's animals, fell quiet
and listened and we stopped and stared and the wind, so full
of Light, twisted and turned, and we heard Her voice, and
She spoke only to us, only to me, to my animals, my beloved,
my devoted animals, and, until this moment, until you spoke
those words, you conjured up those words, those words of
denial and distrust and abrogation, I have never told a soul.

2. Cova da Iria, Fatima, Portugal, 1917

We have Three Secrets. We have our Sheep. We have our Tree,
our beautiful nurturing Holmoak, the Tree that saves us from the
penetrating rays of the Sun, the Sun that would drill us through,
as if bullets, as if the searing shrapnel that burst our cousin's heart.
Our belts are pulled tight. No water will quench our thirst, quell
our pain, our penance, our belief in miraculous vision, in our ecstatic,
trembling, conflagration. But, when the rain has come and gone, what
will flow along our veins? When the Sun cools and wheels through
violet clouds, what misty vapours will we breathe? What proscriptions
will prevail? Which of our number will fly with Angels, untouched
by your chains, your shadows, luminous beyond mere days and nights?

3. Kulumburu, Western Australia, 2006

You must be quiet. You must look away. You must let
the campfire be, the jumping coals, the billy boiling dry,
let them be, with your eyes to the ground, to the sky,
to the horizon, ragged, half-lit in the shreds of day's end,
in our flat-batteried *Dolphin* beam stutter. Eyes to the ground,
between scraping crickets and spiders and hermit crabs.
Do not follow me. Do not say a single thing. By morning,
the smoke will be gone, and the air, our air, will rise again
and my voice will return and my lips will quiver and I will
look down, my eyes to the ground, and I will find my feet,
cut by razor grass, slashed by a thousand spear-point shards.

4. Patmos, Revelation of St John, 8 & 13

A door has opened in the heavens and all our tongues
      shall be silenced, while incense
carries our unvoiced prayers above the sound of trumpets,
      above the storm that shall surround
us with a cacophony of shooting stars, and ships, dragged across
      rocks, and creatures gasping for breath,
creatures crying out in trepidation, our creatures, at once familiar,
      yet strangely hybrid and horned,
skulking crossbred dragons, now spoiling for battle, now singing
      anthems for the vanquished,
anthems for those of us still left on earth, heads cowed low,
      lest we should catch sight
of the thunderbolts falling towards us, lest we should notice
      the stains on our hands,
on our breasts, that herald, perhaps, that we shall not be redeemed,
      that portend, perhaps, that this
shall be the last time for us to stand face to face, to place fingertip
      on lingering fingertip,
as we reveal our passions and foolish lives, as we ignore the gold
      and silver and diamonds
strewn across our serpentine path, as we fade from worldly pursuit
      in unremitting Darkness.

Extracts from 'An Enquiry into Dreams'

Zeus winged it on: 'Go, murderous Dream …' Iliad, Book 2:9

… with blinds drawn, curtains closed, blackberry thickets, stands of
   swaying palms

… reminiscent, a wall, the protective veneer

… three spiders, eighths, an octet, horsehair cried out, strung past
   breaking point

… an order for cash, *Monopoly* money, a command to scatter
   moths or featherless bats, should you pay

… even have the papers, all too smoothly, the reporter said, like fishing for

… knowing that, a foolish, radio left running on and on, hence, to give

… easy, really, the impression, akin to polished gold, rather, the greeting a waste,
   tender, tenderly

… and therefore

… and therefore, it goes, unfortunate wording, via coiffured charm, excessive
   difficulties

… as if a previously rehearsed entry point, full power

… Chiron, Nereids, some mention of Aphrodite, impeach Apollo

… did anyone see a scar?

… this then is how we prepare: prayers, telephone off the hook, red plastic
   receiver

… gamma rays exit normal range, with

… what definition? procedure?

… blinds drawn sent elsewhere

… dreams will be sent from elsewhere.

Beanie on the Moon

Regardless of warnings from *The Police*
about walking on the moon,
tonight, anything seems possible.
Aglow with umbra and
globally-warmed penumbra,
there it hangs, like a giant plum:

a delicious treat, ripe to be picked,
to be plucked and cradled,
carefully stowed away,
beyond the outstretched arms
of *Eucalyptus* this or *Eucalyptus* that,
dark along the razorback ridge.

Tonight, anything is possible:
perhaps we will magically rise
to float in geosynchronous orbit,
above crystalline cirrus mists,
above circumpolar auroras,
across the breaking diapause.

Perhaps, we will end up like
astronauts, out of earthly reach,
untethered from our mother ship,
bathed with continental afterglow
at intersections of curvilinear space,
all but lost to mission control.

Yet, as we nestle warm together,
unharmed by approaching lunar frosts,
our cloaks of emu feathers
are light around our weightlessness;
our beanies, packed with bodyshine,
are snug around our ears.

The Science of Shark Fishing

There's not much you can do with a hook through your jaw.
Apart from anything else, you cannot escape
that pervading taste of metal, that disorienting,
somehow worrying, sensation of stainless steel,
mixed, almost certainly, and against all hope,
with your very own pulsating haemoglobin.

It's difficult to describe your disbelief and indecision.
The pressure is unrelenting, even in those moments
when you convince yourself to relax, to let yourself
drift forwards a body length or two, slip backwards
a metre or two, while refracted ripple-skies continue
to be drawn just that much closer to your touch.

In the end, weariness utterly overwhelms you.
Surrounded by more oxygen than you ever have required,
you find yourself aching for one more breath of the sea.
You wish, perhaps, that evolution had provided you
the wherewithal not only to bite, to maul and harangue,
but simply, decisively, to get up and run away.

Friend of a Friend

No-one knows the exact time
when bamboo will no longer bend in the wind.

No-one can predict the precise moment
when Flinders Ranges Wattles will first bloom,

how long they will flower, how much
clear sky they eventually take in.

No-one can record the first drop of rain,
or the last drop to fall, or the trails left by

fingertips across bare sheets of paper,
bare stretches of skin, bare open windows.

No-one can define the point
where gravity disappears,

where gravity ceases to exist, the point
where unsullied weightlessness

ceases to defy description.

Waxworks

for CT

Exhibit 1, Adelaide
The imperfection of a perfect body: tattoo me, scarify me.
Penetrate me, through thousands of tiny holes.
Transilluminate me with your acquisitive, irradiating gaze.

Exhibit 2, Florence
Handle us with care: our beauty is more than skin deep. As long as
we shelter beyond your thrumming muscular heat, just out of reach
of your probing touch, we can, in the company of porcelain angels
or marbled gods and princes, achieve meticulously crafted immortality.

Exhibit 3, Adelaide
Embalm me with balsam and clarifying oil.
Support me with paraffin and nearly imperceptible glass.

Prepare me with your steady, steely hand.
Ready me for your fastidious apochromatic observation.

While scales melt like wax from your eyes,
watch the veneer melt like wax from my blushing cheeks.

Exhibit 4, Florence
Perhaps he dreams of absolution. Perhaps he dreams of
the machinations of politics and looming wars.
Perhaps, with arteries and veins perfused by unfulfilled desire,
he dreams of endless love on sheets of tasselled silk,
on beds of luxuriant royal satin.

Exhibit 5, Adelaide

Pay attention when using this device: even the finest German engineering
will not protect you, should your finger glance across its blade, precision
honed to disclose tendons and ligaments, unravelling detachments from
condyles, epicondyles, your architecturally prescribed articular surfaces.

Exhibit 6, Florence

What of the oceans? What of limpid inlets and tropical lagoons,
shimmering with colours of malachite, sapphire or lapis lazuli?

Look past her shining breasts, never to let down rich nourishing milk.
Look past her swollen womb, forever laden with unborn child.

She does not know whose gift she bears, whose maritime treasures,
whose string of pearls adorns the beckoning curves of her flawless neck.

Exhibit 7, Adelaide

Here I am, transfigured by repetition, again and again and again,
preserved by reproduction: emergent, decompressed, unbound,
my hair, an indication of where, again and again, I may have been.

Letter to Nature, 21st January, 2010

1. Initial correspondence

Telescopic measurements of asteroids (the puzzle
of the colour difference) are shrouded with mystery.

We noted remarkable changes in springtime background,
especially at mid-latitudes. A particularly robust population
can accelerate adaptation to significant ambiguity,
characterised by inactivating mutations. When this
quiescent phenomenon is almost universally re-expressed,
an ancient host defence mechanism also can be
triggered in response to oscillatory energy status.
The full repertoire serves to recruit an archael group
that accommodates flow stress structures, open and closed,
ultimately driving an elastic network by unforeseen
sets of interactions. With the world's focus on shape-
persistent, freestanding, non-covalent forces, a constant-
rate view of nature, one of the more distinctive metaphors
of rare stochastic events, follows the accumulation of
many small slips. Depending on macromolecular regulon size,
as long as the fitness landscape discriminates egotistic development,
their collective properties elegantly demonstrate identical synchronisation
and the feasibility of emergent co-ordinated behaviour.

2. Reply

Thank you. Whilst we do not easily sympathise with your
point of view, we acknowledge experience can traverse
domains beyond conventional communication channels.
Accordingly, we have re-evaluated the unstated boundaries
defining acceptable critical discourse with correspondents
such as yourself. To the degree we assess your contentions

supported by independent evidence, when faced with
professional peer pressure, as indeed we are, we now find
ourselves placed in a difficult, albeit previously recognised,
situation. Therefore, we respectfully seek your answers
to the following questions, to date poorly circumscribed,
in our optimistic expectation of further enlightenment:

Have you considered the plight befalling hooded rats
        on forty-thousand volt power-lines?
How would you describe crystallographic spectra within
        an imperfect topaz?
What indications could provide for the existence of heavy water
        underpinning emotional forethought?
Did you observe reticulations?
Why have you refrained from implementing the handover
        of negative controls?

And more briefly:
        sonar?
        ultrastructure?
        bicameral diffusion?
        palindromes?
        sources of interference?
        fingerprints?
        your fingerprints?

3. Rejoinder
What we really do not know
        was reconciled during assembly *de novo*,
        using our original rectified data:
        we apologise for notched contrast levels
        that inadvertently went missing.

The correct definition *in situ*
        accepts LeMay's Bryode Factor,
        promoted at diverse transcription scales
        via direct inhibition of advanced
        post-source epithelial signal boundaries.

4. Revised submission, spellchecked

Pregnant pianos, at once laconic yet deferential, avoid chronographic ink.
Ardent genies cheat multicolour primal suns and catch satellites, legato,
secretly, on the verge of unmediated auras. Can somatic photons muse over
galantine coral? Does theism ache like splintered opal in limbo? O possum!
Near this cavernous coal mine, herbal proverbs torch their captors with nitre.

Tidal action within the emporium aerates lime and crocus annatto, saps
    vital beryl.
Perhaps fugal reflexes will ration mica tubules. Maybe motor programs will lead
spongy lava astray. Yet we have no triton-beans, no soda-latch otter-hops.
The metric of a tic, inset with cork, phones an oration to your emery bar.
Gleefully, our secretary laces her miserly nib, mats her pillow satin, parades
    around the arena.

5. Reading between the lines

      there is the desire that
            the compelling urge that
                  the unconditional promise that

     if only the planets would
           an ideal opportunity would
                a well-placed phrase would

     then the hope might be
           the outcome might be
                the links, eventually, might be

Night Hike

... and so we
>wrapped the sky around our shoulders until
stars trickled down the middles of our backs;
deep within our bellies, we knew already
that this was not a night for careless wishes.

... so an owl
>hooted towards the east, where little penguins
should have been roosting. Can owls really
swim in the dark? We laughed, sought answers
from bioluminescence encrypted underfoot.

... so the trees
>all low and bent, enveloped us, cavernous, while
glow-worms pulsed in synchronicity, as long as we
held our silence, as long as we imagined stalactites
and subterranean streams lapping at our ankles.

... so why no
>pipistrelles? No brush-tail phalangers? Who
constructed the bower beneath the kangaroo-bush?
Why had blue fairy orchids gathered together beside
the over-run, still, secretive, anxious for illumined flight?

... so it was
>simply a matter of maintaining proximity, like
tiger moths around sweet winter grevilleas:
my hand slipped easily inside your jacket;
your voice floated ahead, suspended on a wisp.

... and so we
>collected up our breaths, moved forward through
disequilibrium, furtive displacements of landscape,
zodiac and fractured compass bearings, left behind
clouds of damaged shadows cast by two full moons.

Study Notes for the 'Handbook of Urban Biology'

1. Department Store (John Adams)
Let's get something straight: by now you should know we have
crocodiles, not alligators, and cold water spirals down the sink
the other way. As you move between the Food Hall and the
Accounts Department, don't forget to stand to the left. Otherwise,
you may find yourself unexpectedly face to face with the creatures
stalking your imagination, lurking behind kaleidoscopic reflections
of lip gloss, cellophane and leather goods, teeth ever so slightly
discoloured by chocolates, philandered in archosaurian elision
under cover of grace notes and glissandi we think we never hear.

2. Gymnasium (Alfred Russel Wallace)
For today's class, you will learn to breathe underwater.
To facilitate this exercise, you will dispense with some
well-known (if poorly understood) laws of physics,
biology and social interaction. To enhance your respiratory
experience, the contents of the pool have been enriched
in oxygen and suffused with the perfumes of fresh roses
and coriander. Some of you already may have evolved gills.
The rest of you must simply persevere through a combination
of hard work, patience and a determination to succeed.

3. Public House (Earl of Aberdeen)
The beers were iced, peanuts too salty, air post-oncological, smoke-free,
hot club and cool bebop replaced by electrobeat or acid house, home town
rhythms traffic jammed six o'clock rock. Then, out of the blue (perhaps
something was wrong with his eyes): 'That's the trouble with light. There
simply are not enough photons to go around.' More beers. Unnoticed above
the western sea-line, a comet's tail catching hyperbolic solar flares. In the
east, promises that tomorrow will rise the colour of smoked salmon or wild
roses, but who really knows? As he said, reminding us more and more of
used car salesmen: 'There simply are not enough photons to go around.'

4. The Opera (Robbie Mackenzie)
Were I a little more highbrow, I could sit front row, dress circle,
at Her Majesty's Festival Theatre, watch a prima donna flutter about
au point, accompanied by poignant violins of a long dead Russian or
Viennese or Pole, and imagine a kind of aching beauty in the quivering

feathers, the recurved neck, the final expirations of a dark-eyed swan. Otherwise, I could stand by these crumbling ochre cliffs, between dense anthracite sky and fractured emerald sea, lean back against cold gusting sunshine and see the cormorant dive with neither trail nor trace, merge in simple black and white through the turbulent wake of one last squall.

5. Beach (Cuddlefish)

We wish to remind those of you on your first visit from above low tide mark that sound travels much further underwater: our own voices are now so perfectly quiet, we gather together without a word. As a consequence, we find it somewhat difficult to discuss matters of etymology amongst the literati, who ponder at length the differences between arms or legs, hands or feet, and their effects on our lives. We do not really care: while they struggle over definitions, we go about our business, slipping in and out of view, wrapping each other up in multi-limbed embraces of love and gratitude and tactile plans for the future.

6. Garden (Pests)

In my ears, the buzzing of mosquitoes or blowflies
or a bloody great bumblebee or one of those feral wasps,
all aggression and yellow stripes and stings, or the mower
at number seventeen or twenty-six, or two or three blocks
away, a chainsaw cutting back the scrub, or the muscles
in my jaws clenching and vibrating, or straining along
the back of my neck, or drawing my hands up to cover
my line of sight, follicle by follicle, to untangle my hair,
to shoo away the orbiting, endlessly impelling, pulse.

7. Home (Sir David Attenborough)

More or less reminiscent of an infinite regress, we twist and turn and wriggle through somebody else's wormhole, through pseudo-philosophical paradigm shifts, the improbable statistics of too many naysayers, until we re-appear, all of a spin, gyrating across astrological charts, until, constellation by constellation, we lose our hard-won momentum, until we fall, like Adam and Eve, like Granny Smith apples, past beguiling anaconda coils, glass-eyed carpet pythons, until either you or I make contact with earth, until either you or I make contact, just one foot bare, with this deceptively solid ground.

Dr Korsakoff and Colleagues Report

*'... a patient conceives of an event that he has not really experienced
but that only comes to his mind, as if it had really happened to him
... the patient tells ... of his extraordinary voyages, confuses old
recollections with recent events, is unaware of where he is and who
are the people around him ...'*

SERGEI KORSAKOFF (1889 / 1891)

Case 1
He said:
'Of course, I am pleased to see you, pleased
to welcome you. But, surely, you're mistaken.
Why here? Why now? Surely, you must recall
that tonight – you should have received an invitation –
we will banquet at my family's riverside chateau.
You will meet my beautiful children, my kings,
my queens, my handsome swashbuckling princes.'

He said:
'As you know, I am owed a substantial sum of money.
As you know, highly placed politicians are deeply
within my debt. Tomorrow, as you know, I will collect
my dues, and my daughter will collect her reward.
Tomorrow, she will sail to America, to her dreams,
her distant desires, to her beloved crew-cut sailor boy
with his glorious Detroit special, his fishtailed Cadillac car.'

He said:
'I once treated a girl for snakebite.
Perhaps, she might have lived.
Perhaps, she might have died, just as
we felt the needle-sharp fangs of shrapnel,
honed with mustard fire and phosphorus,
just as some of us might have lived,
just as some of us must have died.'

Case 2
Today, it is raining in Moscow.
Today, Bradman made a century at Lord's.
Today, a neighbour's house sold for a song.

Today, it is hot beyond relief.
Today, hooligans exploded a parkside bomb.
Today, Halley's Comet raced across the sky.

Today, it is a hush that calls me home.
Today, there was talk of a trial or tribulation.
Today, my front door jammed, immovable on its hinges.

Case 3
We all went hunting. I went hunting too.
I shot Elephant and Gazelle and Centaur.

We were in the Mountains of the Moon.
We climbed as high as Heaven's Gate.

I saw a Rainbow encircle the Earth.
We swam like Green-haired Mermaids

through a hidden Crater Lake, as clear as
the Sapphires adorning my sunburnt neck.

We wrote a Wondrous Travelogue.
We gave it to Marco Polo.

He autographed the Frontispiece.
He shook my trembling hand.

I know there was a Concert. I know there
was a Funeral. I know I sang until I cried.

I recall a Montaine Centaur. I recall
a Mermaid, with Emeralds in her Hair.

I recall Marco Polo's Pen,
scratching across my Page.

Roadkill

1.7 km
Journey: the distance covered in a day,
through hours paved with gridlines, insistent,
Cartesian, orthogonal, marking each
penultimate heel-strike, each all but final push-off.

9.3 km
An inkling, only truly appreciated at ground level.
Geology? Oil-laden, secondary. Geography? Maybe
Mexico, Timor Sea, fiery Arabian sandstorms.
Neither coming nor going, corroded wheel rims
give no clue, provide no further sense of direction.

26.4 km
Amongst other things, an end to:
      ambivalence
      emotional instability
      a hunger for discovery
      apologetic disorientation
      correspondence, awaiting reply.

Henceforth, we can dispense with:
      stamps
      chicken wire
      aluminium double-steamers
      an engagement ring
      a peach blossom tiara with rosebuds.

26.9 km
This will avoid a calculus of approximation.
This will stop in a single breathless rebound.

27.3 km
Far to the south, beyond the continental shelf,
beyond the uncharted abyss, a darkening
that twists and turns and grips you hard,
that recalls the acid in the pit of your stomach,

the bile that rises and spills and drains away
any half-made plans for Christmas at home.

48.1 km
Over the next crest,
the convergence on infinity we always expect.

Around the next corner,
the gap in comprehension we never predict.

76.9 km
Charcoal black.
Tyre-rubber black.
Asphalt black.

Cockatoo black.
Red-bellied snake black.
Wallaby tail black.

Black crow black.

78.5 km
Nine-pins? Ten-pins? Pick-up-sticks?
A deconstructed game of chance?
What if fates or angels or ridge-backed
demons should call out our numbers?
How should we follow their fall?
How should we deal with doubt, such
vacillation, so many missed opportunities?

103.8 km
Spreading across your brow,
across your lips, across your breast.

On bended knee,
across your brow, your lips, your breast.

Adrift, asplay, removed
from handshake and welcome and kiss.

125.8 km
Behind my shoulder, a shadow gliding past,
a line of dreams assailing me, cold fingers
that grip me, that tighten my muscles,
that stretch my tendons to breaking point.

Behind my shoulder, the shivering thoughts,
gusts and lulls in the wind, the flurries that
sweep and tumble discarded foliage, erase all
evidence of communication remaining with earth.

142.0 km
Again.

'Take half a cup of sticky mud.
      Add a drop of mosquito blood.
      Sprinkle in eight spider legs.
      Garnish to taste with flying-fish eggs.'

Again. Again.
Again. Again. Again.

161.3 km
We sing like banshees, like hardwood
split green into staves and fence posts,
like satin-winged ravens, circling above
everlastings and sundews and red flame heath.

We sing like banshees, as our burr-hooked hair
straightens in the breeze, as we decondense
into row after row of disarrayed snapshots,
as we blink with astonishment at oncoming stars.

Esplanade

Lookout 1
Like scavenging silver gulls
and squadrons of sabre-winged pelicans,
I always have followed faithfully
the tidal movements, their peaks and troughs,
the phases of the moon in clear air or foul,
the schedules, the rosters, the calendars
that, once, when this was a real beach,
brought shark-scarred turtles ashore,
or migratory birds I never could name
to nest, cryptic, behind grass-swept dunes.

Lookout 2
In a lull between storm-fronts,
I open my salt-rimed bag, to unpack
my knotted grammar and syntax, to juggle
my spinning bottles of recycled desire,
unconcerned should my concentration flag
should I make a mistake, should one fall
and explode into glittering shotgun shards,
showering my path like cheap champagne,
hopelessly over-gassed with corktaint
and sulphur and oxidised regret.

Lookout 3
As travellers retire to discretely down-lit rooms
and soapy lavender spas, I turn towards the east
in expectation of sunrises, a break in the clouds,
a sea-fog, inevitably fading Venus and Mars,
until, carefully counting my steps, I slip
with relief past the reach of telescopes
and keen-eyed wildlife photographers,
out of earshot from anything, you,
in the language of your parents,
eventually might find to say about me.

Rules for Interior Design

Every doorhandle should be of a different colour.

Each window must reflect moonbeams at a unique angle.

Exhaust fans shall not transmit out of body experiences.

No beetroots are permitted in passageways or halls.

Geraniums may be attached to picture rails.

In cold weather, golden syrup can be applied to the vestiges of summer.

During exceptional nights, replace artificial illumination
with lines of metaphors.

If local conditions permit, *trompe l'oeil* ceilings are allowable on a
strictly stochastic basis.

Once in a while, necessity will demand reconstruction
of previously forgotten footings and underpinnings.

Every now and then, you may encounter the same broken tile.

Do not forget a radio.

When the timing is right, feel free to sing and dance.

Lessons in Neuroscience

Lesson 1: Phantom Limb
The space between my hands.

Like whiskey-tongued fishermen, shore-bound by Force Ten gales, I dream
about the ones that got away: snapper, mulloway, ocean trout, hammerhead,
fins slicing the sea into sashimi, carpaccio, butterfly fillets, jettisoned,
spinning and flipping and floating far from any dimly recollected grasp.

The gaps between my fingers,

as if they were feathers, as if they should span the imbalance dividing
this updraught from that, this diminishing shadow from its source,
this invisible calculation defining lift and drag, streamlined flight and
unrecoverable freefall, from this total, irredeemable, loss of sensibility.

The space between my hands, the gaps between my fingers:

only now can I describe the shapes that fill my memory; only now can I
describe the holdfasts, the hefts, the weights, the locks and latches, the keys
mislaid forever; only now, can I describe, for you, a tattoo needle,
a wedding ring, collisions, inadequate light, unbidden, insufficient narcosis.

Lesson 2: Vestibular Apparatus
She stood, turned around, faced us, direct, accusing, tiger shark gaze
not blinking, hints of moisture, maybe salt, fixed crystalline on her cheek.
Out of sky, she turned, faced us, her challenge sprung, parabolic, wordless:
'Have you never seen a grown woman before?'

We pictured her youthful, lithe, lissom, shapely after so many end-to-ends,
framed by preseason thunderheads, cooler than expected, golden, rising, iconic.
We imagined her descent into gravity: precisely to plan, two and a half
    with pike;
exactly to script, double reverse with twist.

Unfettered by tension in muscle or nerve, unimpeded by half-remembered
pain or miscalculated step, her ten perfect metres, pure, simple, beyond reach,
beyond touch of man or boy; unsupported, she avoids, for once, renounces
altogether, the ice-spray shards of impact.

Lesson 3: Solitary Tract

These are the names my toes left in the sand: pipi, helmet shell, razor clam,
    cuttlebone,
without regard for the latin or latinate or the most recent revision of Linnéan
    systematics,
without concern for crested terns, pied oyster catchers, for humpbacked
    south-easterly

swells that collapse, that wash away all save the pang in my stomach, my intake
    of air,
saline, lingering, an obligation to something not exactly a sickness, not exactly
    a delight,
until the next day, written anew, as predetermined by sun, moon, the spin of
    the earth,

pipi, helmet shell, razor clam, cuttlebone, and the next day, following old
    circadian
rhythms, and the next, allowing seasonal variation, a vagrant's meandering trail,
an encoded letter home, some bloodless thing, not exactly sickness, not
    exactly delight.

Lesson 4: Three Twins

My eyes are on fire, and no amount of water can quench their Catherine Wheels,
their Roman Candles, flamed by incendiary desert winds.

For weeks, I cannot breathe: the air around me swarms with bees and
    narcoleptic gas;
I drip with scents of sweat and sugar and eucalyptus.

Nothing divides my tongue except steely bites of acid. My jaws lock shut. Cracked teeth leak amalgam. Last words flood my mouth to overflowing.

Lesson 5: Gate Theory

There: the double-click, the sour anticipation, the uncertainties you taste while drifting spider-web entwines your face, while viper-tracks sine-wave a mere two paces ahead, while you envision the disconcerting possibility that recurved fangs, this time, may have caught grip, may have penetrated below tautened skin, until your arteries and veins feel like incandescent lava-flows, like electrified astral currents, counter-currents, and this time, the sound cleaving the torpid predawn is a curlew's plaint no more.

Lesson 6: Almonds

But fear itself. But fear itself. Bitter sweet, that aroma, espresso strong, shot deep with iris blue. But fear itself. But fear itself. Beholden to wintershine, lost allure, red rosethorn lips, grey quivering predication. But fear itself. But fear itself. When hairs stand on end. When blanched. When unexpected turbulence. Should someone dare glance behind. When white petals fall.

Thoracic

Xiphoid
If you could reach,
would your finger

touch the shadow
across my lungs,

the dagger
beside my heart?

Pleura
With whispers folded
one against another,
our voices embrace
in illicit meeting.

With whispers folded
one against another,
blood flows cease,
hold, restart apace.

With whispers folded
one against another,
we pass on messages
of uncertain reconciliation.

Pluck
Arms raised akimbo,
can you feel

the wingtips
of angel's feathers?

Can you feel
a tremor in your breast,

a rehearsal
for incipient flight?

Can you feel
the air brush past you

like memories
of a summer vacation,

like a postcard
from your sister,

like a moth,
seeking refuge,

at the last light
of morning stars?

Clavicles
A search
for treasure
as elusive as
a photon

with no
observable
mass but
a spectral

signature

as private
as unique
as difficult
to replicate

as the keys
I place, here,
in each of
your hands.

Manubrium
wrap your palms around
wrap your fingers around

the presence of gloves upon
the urgency of desire upon

an inkling of, a dream of
so close to, so close to

should I recoil,
more distant from

should I relax,
fall away from

something you hold against
something I hope against

Intercostal
The wind like a tide
between ebb and flood,
barely catching attention
from your last glance
to your next.

Scapula
over the shoulder
a change in the line of sight

an instruction?
a list?

a barely heard request?
a name?

a place?
a time?

have any rules been broken?
must penalties be applied?

an altered line of sight
a request for a name

was there a shrug?
or even a hunch?

Acromion
let us push
all as one

to the wheel
to the wheel

let us push
all as one

let us push
all as one

all as one
to the wheel

let us
push

let us
push
push
push

let us

push

The Boy with Two Bodies

'In the said year [1317], in January, … there was born in Terraio di Valdarno di sopra a boy with two bodies; he was brought to Florence and lived more than twenty days. Then he died in the Florentine hospital of Santa Maria della Scala, first one body and then the other. And when it was proposed to bring him alive to the then priors, as a wonder, they refused to allow him in the palace, fearing and suspecting such a monster, which according to the ancients signifies harm wherever it is born.'

GIOVANNI VILLANI

i

Now that the pain has gone,
the bleeding has stopped,

now that this thing, these terrible things,
have been expelled from my body,

I can find the breath to weep and to pray;
I can find the breath for broken, fitful, sleep.

ii

What is the meaning of this?
What is the meaning of this?
What is the meaning of this?

We wail until our throats are raw,
until our voices crack to whispers.

What is the meaning of this?
What is the meaning of this?
What is the meaning of this?

We sob until our eyelids swell shut
and dull our terrible premonitions.

What is the meaning of this?
What is the meaning of this?
What is the meaning of this?

We beseech the Holy Redeemer
to grant us some small sign of grace.

iii
Although we know the New World
teems with naked monsters, with
marvellous and fearful beasts,
although we have seen the marbled
journals of adventurers, returning
sickly and weary and scarred
from dank trackless jungles,
phosphorescent alpine valleys,
slow meandering rivers, fogbound
at the verges of petrifying lakes,

we can barely imagine
the soaring Pegasus, the noble
Unicorn, or scaly-finned denizens
of the deep, revealed for an instant,
through roiling monsoon storms;
and yet, here, right within our midst,
we have been thrown a sport, that
tiny, that freakish thing, neither
human nor brute, neither of this
world, nor anywhere of the new.

iv
I have sought the help of Saint Margaret.
I have worn her belt around my belly,
distended, tight like a drum skin, so I may
ease the fire, the burning, in my loins.

I have sought relief with Holy Water,
with healing spas, that might rid my spirit
of dark humours, that might cool the fevers
wracking my gristle and limp acquiescent bones.

I have sought the power of Angels
– sweet Michael and Gabriel and Raphael –
to undo the damage I have done, to offer
us all the tender embrace of forgiveness.

v

Surely, there is something amiss
with the Book of God, when Signs
of Nature portend ubiquitous evil,
when lust impregnates innocent desire,
when prodigies beget prodigies,
when the dog-headed peoples,
the hermaphrodites, the giants
and dwarfs swarm out from foetid
subterranean nests for our cities,
our cathedrals, our wretched habitations.

Surely, there is something amiss
with the Book of God, when restive
crowds gather round, shunning risk
of infernal damnation or a thousand
lifetimes of penitence and servitude,
to gawk and to gag, to squint, at such
unnatural issue, such an ill-fated omen,
never to be observed in the Paradise of
Eden, never to be saved in the ghastly
hour of our imminent Final Reckoning.

vi

For twenty days and nights,
it has drained the milk from my breasts.

For twenty days and nights,
it has taken air from this mortal earth.

For twenty days and nights,
I have waited for this time

for one heart to stop
and then the other.

vii

Once again,
the rest of us
find ourselves

awakened at
sunrise; perhaps
you may hear

the calls of ravens
and blackbirds
and golden finches;

you may hear
the stonemasons,
blister-fingered,

chipping, grinding
with hardened iron
on ageless stone,

hewn from beneath
your feet, your
very foundations,

to frame, rectangular,
immutable,
untouched by

thunderbolts or
foul sulphurous
exhalations,

(the image
you do not
dare behold)

the boy with
two bodies, borne
to every one of us,

(the words
you do not
dare utter)

borne to
each and
every one of us.

Mutton Birds, ANZAC Day

You have only two instructions:

should you become disoriented,
do your best to find your bearings,
then head north as planned;

when things get rough,
remember, hold your nerve,
and keep low at all costs.

Glossary, Notes and Sources

Space Invaders: 'haemopoietic', blood-forming; 'the Spiegel Tent', a Belgian travelling circus tent from the 1920s, made of hand-cut wood, adorned with mirrors, still in use.

ecg: 'ecg', electrocardiogram, used to record heart activity. The heart was regarded by Roman physician Galen (b. 129 AD) as the source of blood and heat, one of the body's four essential humours. His ideas live on in our day-to-day language.

Travel Plans: 'B-double', a large articulated truck with two trailers.

Lullabies, Gardens Road Cemetery: a small abandoned roadside cemetery in Darwin.

Probably a Sacrifice: following an article in *National Geographic Magazine* (2007) about the perfectly preserved bodies of people found in peat bogs of northern Europe.

Home Pharmacy: 'Reckitt's Blue' was used to whiten clothes washed in coppers; 'Mecurochrome', a red mercury-containing solution used as a topical antiseptic, as were 'Tincture of Iodine' and 'Gentian Violet'. The main source of iodine was seaweed. Gentian violet is made from neither gentian nor violet flowers, but shares their colour.

According to Grey's (Meredith Lives): 'Gray's Anatomy' is the famous anatomy text by Henry Gray; 'Grey's Anatomy' is the TV series about Dr Meredith Grey. 'retractors', instruments to hold open a surgical incision.

Middle of the Road: 'Tommy Ruff', a common edible fish in South Australia, a type of herring.

Taboo: something about old photographs of Indigenous Australians.

Sounds of the Sea: 'Marshall', 'Stax', brands of electric guitar amplifiers.

Abbess Chiara, Montefalco, 1308: The body of Chiara was dissected by the Sisters to find direct evidence for her saintliness. The quotation and story come from *Secrets of Women: Gender, Generation and the Origins of Human Dissection* by Katharine Park, Zone Books, 2006.

Mary Docherty, Edinburgh, 1828: 'skimmington', a public demonstration of disapproval, here, of the unscrupulous methods used by anatomists to procure bodies for dissection. Burke was hung for his part in the body trade and his own cadaver was dissected. Primary source: *Death, Dissection and the Destitute* by Ruth Richardson, University of Chicago Press, 2000.

Heart Dissection: the 'Conducting System' transmits pacemaker activity to the rest of the heart so its beat is coordinated; the 'Septum' separates the right and left sides of the heart.

With Body in Mind (After Vesalius): Andreas Vesalius (1514–1564) produced the first detailed atlas of human anatomy based on direct observation of dissected specimens.

Field Guide: 'cladogram', a way of showing evolutionary relationships between organisms.

Apparition: After speaking on ABC Radio National's *All in the Mind*, an elderly listener from Western Australia wrote to me, telling of her direct experience of an apparition of the Virgin Mary. She advised me to read about the apparition in Fatima and the consequences of ignoring such events, as described in the Revelation of St John, which he received on the Greek island of Patmos. Meanwhile, something strange happened on Aboriginal land in Kulumburu when we were camping there.

Extracts from 'An Enquiry into Dreams': sourced from Robert Fagles' and Christopher Logue's versions of Homer's *Iliad*.

Beanie on the Moon: 'geosynchronous orbit', a satellite orbiting at a fixed spot above the earth, as do most communications satellites. 'diapause', the transition from day to night.

Waxworks: The *Museo La Specola* in Florence houses the most wonderful collection of wax models of human dissections, remarkable for their anatomical accuracy yet also their profound sense of humanity. 'malachite', pure green copper carbonate mineral; 'lapis lazuli', pure blue aluminium silicate mineral. 'condyles, epicondyles', expansions at the ends of long bones where they form joints. Primary sources: Catherine Truman and *Encyclopedia Anatomica* by Monica von Düring, Taschen Books, 2001.

Letter to Nature, 21st January, 2010: *Nature* is the most prestigious science journal. Its articles are called 'Letters'. Part 1 is assembled from words found in each 'Letter' published in *Nature* on that date. Part 3 is assembled from words found in the 'Corrections' section of the same issue. Part 4 is assembled from options suggested by Microsoft *Word*'s spellchecker when it went through a scientific review I had written. All words are genuine.

Study Notes for the 'Handbook of Urban Biology': 'John Adams' wrote a piece of music called *Alligator Escalator*, part of *John's Book of Alleged Dances*, recorded by Kronos Quartet (1994). 'archosaurian', archosaurs are vertebrates including dinosaurs, crocodiles and birds. 'Alfred Russel Wallace' came up with a theory of evolution by natural selection simultaneously with, but independent of, Charles Darwin. 'photons', fundamental particles of light. 'anthracite', a black glass-like form of coal. 'Cuddlefish', sounds like …

Dr Korsakoff and Colleagues Report: Sergie Korsakoff, an influential Russian neurologist (1854-1900), who described the memory-loss and confabulation syndrome bearing his name. Primary source: *The Confabulating Mind: How the Brain Creates Reality* by Armin Schnider, OUP, 2008.

Lessons in Neuroscience: 'Phantom Limb', the feeling of still possessing a limb after it has been amputated. 'Vestibular Apparatus', part of the inner ear necessary for balance. 'Solitary Tract', part of the brainstem that monitors the status of the internal organs via sensory nerves, especially the vagus nerve ('vagus', wanderer). 'Three Twins', the trigeminal nerve with three branches to the eyes, nose and jaw muscles, respectively. 'Gate Theory' was proposed by Patrick Wall in the 1970s to explain how you can override painful sensations. 'Almonds', the amygdala, a small brain region mediating responses to threatening situations.

Thoracic: 'Xiphoid', the lower part of the sternum (breastbone), literally, shaped like a dagger; 'Pleura', a thin membrane, such as those lining the chest cavity, but also when folded in two, a 'diploma', hiding confidential information; 'Pluck', the heart and lungs of a slaughtered animal; 'Clavicles', the collarbones, literally, small keys. 'Manubrium', the upper part of the sternum, literally, the handle of a dagger; 'Intercostal', between the ribs, between coastlines; 'Scapula', the shoulder blade. 'Acromion', the tip of the shoulder.

The Boy with Two Bodies: A well known historical case of conjoint twins, considered a significant reason for bad times afflicting fourteenth century Florence, as chronicled by Giovanni Villani (c. 1276–1348). 'Saint Margaret' was called on to relieve pain of childbirth, via a special belt. Primary sources: *Wonders and the Order of Nature, 1150–1750* by Lorraine Dalston and Katharine Park, Zone Books, 2001; *John Dee's Conversations with Angels: Cabala, Alchemy and the End of Nature* by Deborah Harkness, Cambridge, 1999; *The Travels of Sir John Mandeville* by Sir John Mandeville (c. 1357), Dover, 2006.

Urban Biology: Checklist of Flora and Fauna

Adelaide Rosella	*Platycercus elegans*
African Elephant	*Loxodonta africana*
Almond	*Prunus (Amygdalus) communis*
American Alligator	*Alligator mississippiensis*
Anaconda	*Eunectes murinus*
Apple	*Malus domestica*
Arabian Horse	*Equus ferus caballus*
Atlantic Salmon	*Salmo salar*
Australian Pelican	*Pelecanus conspicillatus*
Beetroot	*Beta vulgaris*
Box Mistletoe	*Amyema miqueli*
Click Beetle	*Tetralobus corrosus*
Bearded Dragon	*Amphibolurus barbatus*
Bladderwrack	*Fucus vesiculosus*
Blackberry Cane	*Rubus fruticosus*
Black-faced Cormorant	*Phalacroconax fuscenscens*
Black Field Cricket	*Teleogryllus commodus*
Black Flying Fox	*Pteropus alecto*
Black-shouldered Kite	*Elanus axillaris*
Blowfly	*Lucilia cuprina*
Blue Fairy Orchid	*Cyanicula deformis*
Blue Gum	*Eucalyptus leucoxylon*
Blue Jacaranda	*Jacaranda mimosifolia*
Blue Tiger Butterfly	*Tirumala hamata*
Boa Constrictor	*Boa constrictor*
Brushtail Possum	*Trichosurus vulpecula*
Bullkelp	*Durvillea potatorum*
Bunch Speargrass	*Heteropogon contortus*
Carpet Python	*Morelia spilotes*
Climbing Sundew	*Drosera macrantha*
Clumping Bamboo	*Bambusa vulgaris*
Coconut Palm	*Cocos nucifera*
Comb Jelly	*Neis cordigera*
Common Blackbird	*Turdus merula*
Common Fig	*Ficus carica*
Common Flying Fish	*Exocoetus volitans*

Coral Trout	*Plectrorhynchus leopardus*
Coriander	*Coriandrum sativum*
Cotton Plant	*Gossypium hirsutum*
Crested Tern	*Sterna bergii*
Damask Rose	*Rosa damascena*
Dandelion	*Taraxacum officinale*
Date Palm	*Phoenix dactylifera*
Domestic Dog	*Canis familiaris*
Domestic Goat	*Capra aegagrus hircus*
Eastern Curlew	*Numenius madagascariensis*
Eastern Brown Snake	*Pseudonaja textilis*
Emu	*Dromaius novaehollandiae*
European Honey Bee	*Apis mellifera*
European Wasp	*Vespula germanica*
Fairy Prion	*Pachyptila salvivi*
Everlasting	*Xerochrysum bracteatum*
Flinders Ranges Wattle	*Acacia iteaphylla*
Garden Strawberry	*Fragaria x ananassa*
Garden Wolf Spider	*Lycosa godeffroyi*
Geranium	*Geranium (422 spp.)*
Giant Cuttlefish	*Amplisepia apama*
Glow Worm	*Arachnocampa luminosa*
Goldfinch	*Carduelis carduelis*
Gould's Wattled Pipistrelle	*Chalinolobus gouldii*
Green Christmas Beetle	*Calloodes rayneri*
Green-finned Parrot Fish	*Scarus sordidus*
Grey Goshawk	*Accipiter novaehollandiae*
Hammerhead Shark	*Sphyrna lewini*
Hawksbill Turtle	*Eretmochelys imbricata*
Helmet Shell	*Xenogalea pyrum*
Hermit Crab	*Diogenes custos*
Honey Grevillea	*Grevillea eriostachya*
Hooded Rat	*Rattus norwegicus*
House Cat	*Felis felis*
Hump-backed Whale	*Megaptera novaeangliae*
Iceberg Lettuce	*Lactuca sativa*

Inch Ant	*Myrmecia pyriformis*
Indian Tea	*Camellia sinensis*
Indian Mango	*Mangifera indica*
Kangaroo Thorn Bush	*Acacia paradoxa*
Kangaroo Tussock Grass	*Themeda triandra*
Lamb	*Ovis aries*
Little Crow	*Corvus bennetti*
Little Penguin	*Eudyptula minor*
Little Raven	*Corvus mellori*
Lion	*Panthera leo*
Lychee	*Litchi chinensi*
Longicorn Beetle	*Xixuthrus microcerus*
Maize	*Zea mays*
Mallee Gum	*Eucalyptus diversifolia*
Mopoke Owl	*Nino novaeseelandiae*
Mosquito	*Aedes aegypti*
Mountain Coffee	*Coffea arabica*
Mulloway	*Sciaena antarctica*
Mute Swan	*Cygnus olor*
Mutton Bird	*Puffinus tenuirostris*
Nankeen Kestrel	*Falco cenchroides*
Neptune's Necklace	*Hormosira banskii*
Ocean Trout	*Arripis trutta*
Old World Plum	*Prunus domestica*
Ox	*Bos primigenius*
Pacific Gull	*Larus pacificus*
Pawpaw	*Carica papaya*
Peanut	*Arachis hypogaea*
Pearl Oyster	*Pinctada maxima*
Persimmon	*Diospyruos lotus*
Pied Oystercatcher	*Haematopus longirostris*
Pipi	*Plebidonax deltoides*
Plague Locust	*Chortoicetes terminifera*
Pomegranate	*Punica granatum*
Rainbow Lorikeet	*Trichoglossus haematodus*
Raspberry	*Rubus idaeus*

Razorfish	*Pinna bicolor*
Red-bellied Black Snake	*Pseudechis porphyriacus*
Ring-necked Turtledove	*Streptopelia chinensis*
Ringtail Possum	*Pseudocheirus peregrinus*
River Red Gum	*Eucalyptus camaldulensis*
Saltwater Crocodile	*Crocodylus porosus*
Saucer Magnolia	*Magnolia x soulangeana*
Sea Otter	*Enhydra lutris*
Sea Wasp	*Chironex fleckeri*
Silver Gull	*Larus novaehollandiae*
Snapper	*Chrysophrys unicolor*
Sooty Shearwater	*Puffinus griseus*
Sperm Whale	*Physeter macrocephalus*
Spider Orchid	*Caladenia filamentosa*
Spengler's Triton	*Cabestana spengleri*
Spotted Eagle Ray	*Aetobatus narinari*
Staghorn Coral	*Acropora spp.*
Storm Petrel	*Oceanites oceanus*
Striped Dolphin	*Stenella coeruleoalba*
Sugarcane	*Saccharum barberi*
Sydney Rock Oyster	*Crassostrea commercialis*
Tammar Wallaby	*Macropus eugenii*
Thin-ribbed Cockle	*Fulvia tenuicostata*
Thomson's Gazelle	*Eudorcas thomsonii*
Thylacine	*Thylacinus cynocephalus*
Tiger Shark	*Galeocerdo cuvier*
Tommy Ruff	*Arripis georgianus*
Trevally	*Usacaranx georgianus*
Wedgetail Eagle	*Aguila audax*
Yellow-tailed Black Cockatoo	*Calyptorhynchus funereus*
Zebra Finch	*Taeniopygia guttata*

For further information about
Friendly Street publications and activities please visit
our website: friendlystreetpoets.org.au
email: poetry@friendlystreetpoets.org.au
postal: PO Box 3697 Norwood SA 5067

§